HR: Making Change Happen

Dr Eamonn Molloy
Professor Richard Whittington

The Chartered Institute of Personnel and Development is the leading publisher of books and reports for personnel and training professionals, students, and all those concerned with the effective management and development of people at work. For full details of all our titles, please contact the Publishing Department:

Tel: 020 8612 6204

E-mail: publish@cipd.co.uk

To view and purchase all CIPD titles:
www.cipd.co.uk/bookstore

For details of CIPD research projects:
www.cipd.co.uk/research

HR: Making Change Happen

Dr Eamonn Molloy
Professor Richard Whittington

Saïd Business School, University of Oxford

First published 2005
Reprinted 2005, 2006, 2008
Cover design by Curve
Designed by Beacon GDT
Typeset by Paperweight
Printed in Great Britain by Short Run Press

British Library Cataloguing in Publication Data
A catalogue record for this book is available from the British Library

ISBN 1 84398 113 0
ISBN-13 978 1 84398 113 8

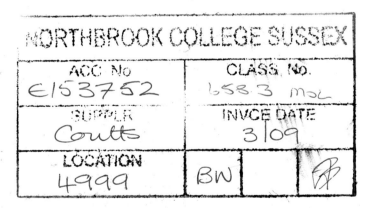

Chartered Institute of Personnel and Development,
151 The Broadway, London SW19 1JQ

Tel: 020 8612 6200
Website: www.cipd.co.uk

Incorporated by Royal Charter. Registered charity no. 1079797.

Contents

Acknowledgements

The CIPD would like to thank Dr Eamonn Molloy and Professor Richard Whittington of Saïd Business School for managing and preparing this Executive Briefing.

The organisations that kindly contributed to the case studies used in this Executive Briefing included:

CACHE

Cadbury Schweppes

Lever Fabergé

Lewisham Borough Council

National Health Service

Nationwide

Northamptonshire County Council

National Open College Network

Ordnance Survey

United Utilities

The members of the project's steering group (detailed below) are also thanked for their contributions.

John Ainley	General Insurance, Norwich Union
Chris Bones	Cadbury Schweppes
Dr Aysen Broadfield	GE Capital
Andrew Campbell	Ashridge Strategic Management Centre
Jane Cotton	Oxfam
Andreas Ghosh	Lewisham Council
Chris Goscomb	Shell
Jan Hutchinson	Ordnance Survey
Dr Sheryll Kennedy	Kennedy Business Development
John Lee	Martlet Business Services
Dr Clive Morton	The Morton Partnership
Andrew Newall	Allied Domecq
Agnes Roux-Kiener	Unilever
David Shaw	PwC Consulting
Mike Staunton	Interbrew
David Smith	Asda

List of figures and tables

Foreword

Against evidence of a history of poor change management in large organisations, due, in part at least, to lack of effective people management, and to a failure to recognise change management as a management science in its own right, the CIPD embarked upon a three-year project, *Organising For Success*, in 2002. The research is being undertaken on behalf of the Institute by a team of researchers led by Richard Whittington, Professor of Strategy and Organisation at the Saïd Business School, University of Oxford.

The focus of this three-year CIPD project is the relationships between business strategy, organisational structures and processes, people management policies and the work of the HR professional, and business performance. The aims of the research have been to:

- review current trends in organisational structure and design and summarise existing knowledge about the practice of organisational restructuring, identifying knowledge and practice gaps

- identify current and emerging forms of organisation

- provide understanding of and guidance on the practice of organisational restructuring, and in particular the capabilities required for effective restructuring, to deliver improved business performance

- raise awareness about, and influence practice in, effective organisational restructuring among senior executives

- analyse the contribution of effective people management for effective restructuring

- draw conclusions and provide recommendations that support CIPD members in improving their contribution to the practice of organisational restructuring.

In order to undertake the work the following research methodology was agreed:

- an external steering group for the project

- a review of current published and unpublished material on new forms of organising

- two major surveys of recent and current experience of reorganising in over 800

UK-based organisations, including responses from chief executives, HR directors, IT, operational and finance directors

◘ in-depth case studies examining specific reorganisations within eleven organisations.

Since the outset of the project, the CIPD has published a series of research reports, surveys and articles addressing these different aims, including:

◘ *Organising For Success in the Twenty-First Century: A starting point for change* (2002) by Richard Whittington and Michael Mayer

◘ *Reorganising for Success: CEOs' and HR Managers' Perceptions.* Survey report, 2003

◘ *HR and Reorganisation – Managing the challenge of change* (2004). A change agenda

◘ *Reorganising for Success: A survey of HR's role in change.* Survey report, 2004.

In advance of the final comprehensive project report, this current Executive Briefing is intended to meet the third and fourth project aims in particular. It is designed to provide practical ideas, tools and tips for people management and development professonals on how to influence and implement restructuring and change effectively. It summarises key common lessons learned to date from all the research, with particular focus on lessons learned from the 11 organisations involved as case study participants.

In so doing, this publication's target audience is those HR development and business executives who both wish to enhance their understanding of managing change and who wish to contribute more effectively to their organisation's change initiatives.

A key finding from all the CIPD's business and organisational research is the importance of tailoring approaches to suit the goals and character of each organisation. Any guidance has to acknowledge the fine balance between being over-prescriptive and being too general to provide any meaningful practical guidance. The use of extensive case study material in the Briefing is intended to demonstrate the appropriateness of different responses in different contexts. Although it cannot endeavour to provide universal solutions, we hope its examples and ideas will help readers to address their own particular situations.

The research findings to date demonstrate that every large organisation is having to reorganise regularly. The drivers for change are wide-ranging and well publicised, including competition in the private sector, and increased efficiency in the public sector. HR changes themselves can be massive – for example, the NHS Agenda for Change. Yet 40 per cent of changes fail to meet their objectives. We believe that people management and development professionals have a major contribution to make in improving the success and practice of reorganising, which will benefit company performance, their employees and their customers.

Our subsequent final research report will pull together the main conclusions from this three-year project. The CIPD will then be working hard to ensure that these conclusions are translated into the effective practice of organisational restructuring to which people management and development professionals can contribute significantly.

Do let us have your reactions to our findings and tell us about your own experiences so that we can continue to add to our body of knowledge on successful reorganising.

Vanessa Robinson
Adviser, Organisation and Resourcing
Chartered Institute of Personnel and Development
(v.robinson@cipd.co.uk)

Executive summary

This Executive Briefing by the Chartered Institute of Personnel and Development (CIPD) draws upon two surveys and 11 in-depth case studies of organisational restructuring, reform and change conducted over a period of two and a half years. From the research, the briefing identifies seven key areas of activity that make successful change happen – the seven Cs of change.

Figure 1 | The seven Cs of change

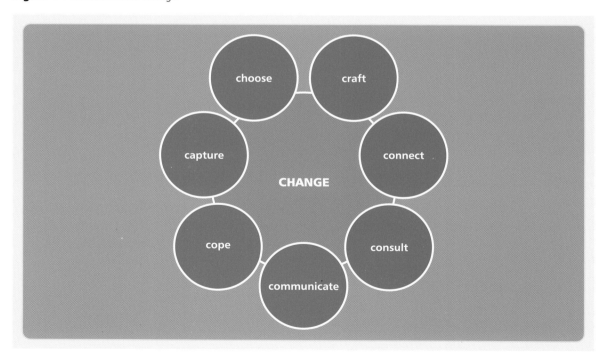

Choosing a team: being a team

Choosing the right team to make change happen is critical. Managing change requires leadership and different mixes of skill, capability and experience at different phases. Key skills highlighted by participants in our research are:

- managing organisational culture

- organisational design

- project management

- political astuteness.

The team must ensure sustained senior management support in terms of resources, organisational politics and the clear setting of objectives. HR plays a key role in both choosing the team, whether sourced internally or externally, and as an essential member of the change team itself. HR professionals are identified by chief executives and management colleagues as highly valued members of the typical reorganisation team.

Crafting the vision and the path

Change needs direction, and as with any journey, it helps to plan the route. Setting realistic and achievable objectives requires effort, skill and commitment to define. Successful change draws upon project management disciplines. However, our survey evidence suggests that more than half of change projects fail to use disciplined project management and project management skills were lacking in almost half of all change initiatives – a key contributor to the failure to achieve planned objectives.

Connecting organisation-wide change

Effective reorganisation avoids piecemeal approaches to change, setting restructuring within the organisation-wide context. Changes of systems, structures and the 'soft' people-related and cultural aspects of the organisation must be carefully synchronised with each other and with the overall strategy. For example, restructuring initiatives must give due attention to the effects on career and reward systems. HR professionals have a key role in championing the people agenda in this respect, and developing and implementing appropriate supporting processes.

Consulting stakeholders

Successful change requires real consultation with all key stakeholders, most notably affected employees. One-way information provision is not enough to win support for change and can often isolate key stakeholders. HR professionals have a responsibility to make sure that employees, unions and other stakeholders, including customers and suppliers, are meaningfully consulted and involved. Employee involvement in change, however, must take place in the context of clearly defined milestones and rigorous project management.

Communicating

It is critical that the rationale for, design of, timing of, and implications of change are completely understood by everyone affected by it, including employees, customers and suppliers. There is a vast range of communication strategies and techniques available, and choosing the right techniques at the right time is an important capability. Communication has to be accurate, meaningful, regular, transparent, consistent, coherent, up-to-date and cascaded throughout the organisation.

Coping with change

Change can be stressful both for those affected by it and for those that are making it happen. People tend to pass through a cycle of emotions when experiencing change, and knowledge of this cycle can help manage some of the issues that might arise. Effective change managers anticipate potential problems related to coping with change and put in place mechanisms for dealing with them – another important role for people management and development professionals.

Capturing learning

Successful restructuring and change relies on change team members bringing deep experience and knowledge of change from both within and outside of the organisation. HR professionals are often crucial carriers of this knowledge, being directly involved in change more frequently than their peers and being well connected with outside organisations. Better results are achieved where these skilled and experienced teams also seek additional knowledge and experience elsewhere, both inside their own organisation and externally, particularly from outside their own sector. Capturing and disseminating knowledge and information is an effective learning and risk management technique that the most successful organisations employ extensively.

- HR is a key player in making change happen.

- Organisations are experiencing high-frequency rates of change.

- Involving employees in change supports implementation.

1 | Introduction: the seven Cs of change

It is only when you work out the things you need to do to get from the current position to the desired position that you realise that doing all these requires organisation. It may be that some people can visualise what the new organisation should be, but they sure as hell cannot hold all the balls in the air to get them there.

Human resource director,
multinational company

Organising for Success is a three-year research programme consisting of two surveys and 11 case studies of reorganising practice. This Executive Briefing draws upon findings from both surveys and the case studies. The first and second survey reports are available from the CIPD (CIPD, 2003; 2004) and the comprehensive final report from the project will be available in Spring 2005.

In this Executive Briefing we draw upon the Organising for Success research project to provide an overview of current approaches to change, as well as the most important lessons learned from those people who have managed major organisational changes. The Briefing is not a formula or 'how-to' manual for managers. Instead, it is designed to be informative and to highlight the key issues and challenges that arise in

managing for change and some common methods for addressing them.

In communicating the experiences and learning collected through the research, it is hoped that this Briefing will help managers to plan, manage and implement organisational changes more effectively and avoid some of the traps inherent in managing reorganisations. Each chapter focuses on the key activities and requirements that make change happen successfully in organisations.

> *'...organisations are experiencing high-frequency rates of change. Yet the language of change management is far from universal.'*

In today's fast-paced world, organisations are experiencing high-frequency rates of change. Yet the language of change management is far from universal. Many different kinds of organisational change occur – for example, restructuring, reorganisation, culture change, each of which may mean slightly different things to different people.

The change programmes, projects, restructuring and reorganisations that we were fortunate enough to be able to study, and the responses to our surveys, indicated that in practice these terms are often used interchangeably. It is not the aim of this Briefing to attempt to resolve these differences. Rather we are interested in the broader lessons from making change happen. In light of this, we use the terms 'change' and 'change management' to encompass reorganisation, restructuring, culture change, process change and technology change.

We recognise that this is a broad sweep, but a key aim of this Briefing is to emphasise the similarities between approaches to change management and the importance of integrating different kinds of change. From the surveys and case studies we identified seven key areas of action for making change happen – the seven Cs of successful change. This Briefing discusses each of the seven Cs in turn, and concludes with a final chapter highlighting the role of HR professionals in relation to each one.

> '*We have known for many years that involving employees in change initiatives supports acceptance and effective implementation. Yet many employers still ignore the basic precept.*'

The seven Cs of change

Our work highlights the following key requirements of successful change:

- choosing a team: being a team

- crafting the vision and path

- connecting organisation-wide change

- consulting stakeholders

- communicating

- coping with change

- capturing learning.

Although we have found that the practices of change management across different kinds of change have a lot in common, so too do some of the challenges. The same technology, tools and techniques can be applied in many different ways, successfully or unsuccessfully. While many of these other areas were superficially fairly obvious, we have found that ignorance in practice of them, or failures to address them successfully, help to explain the continuing high failure rates with organisational change initiatives.

Take employees themselves: issues of employee resistance to change are often present, yet these can be handled well or badly. We have known for many years that involving employees in change initiatives supports acceptance and effective implementation. Yet many employers still ignore the basic precept. Most managers know that change projects can suffer from scope creep, run over budget or lose momentum as 'initiative fatigue' sets in. Yet basic project management disciplines are ignored in a surprising number of instances.

Achieving the appropriate balance between all the various elements and phases of reorganisation requires sophisticated management capability. By focusing on key activities in making change happen, we hope that this Briefing will help achieve that balance and help organisations manage and deliver effective reorganisations and reforms more successfully.

- ◘ **Leadership and senior management team are vital.**

- ◘ **Balance between in-house staff and external consultants needs to be struck.**

- ◘ **Strong programme and project management skills are needed.**

2 | Choosing a team: being a team

If you want to get something to really stick and happen, you have to start at the top – you have to start with the boardroom.

Change programme director,
multinational company

This section focuses on the practitioners of change, the people who make change happen. Different people are required for different roles at different phases of change – from vision through to implementation. The aim of this section is to provide a general overview of how change activities and roles interrelate. It is not intended to be a complete checklist of all the roles and tasks involved. More important is to consider and anticipate the different mix of skills that are needed. In managing change successfully it is critical that everyone concerned is clear about what is required of them and for how long – in other words, how their role fits with the overall plan for delivering change.

Project teams and others involved in managing change – for example, specialist external consultants – have to work closely as a coherent network of skilled resources in order to deliver effective change. In the following sections we discuss the responsibilities of some key groups.

Towards the end of this section we illustrate the different choices that two of our case studies made in putting together the optimal team for their change projects.

Top team

A very clear message from both our case studies and the surveys was that change is most likely to deliver success when there is strong leadership and senior management team sponsorship. However, it was reported that leadership support for change was insufficient in 41 per cent of cases, and – as a change manager in one of our case studies ominously put it –

If you haven't got commitment from the senior management team, you are basically down a black hole…

The top team must lead by example, by 'living' new ways of working, exhibiting new behaviours while continuing their responsibilities for business as usual, our research participants told us. There is a lot to be said for acting as if the changes have already taken place. This sends a strong message to people in the organisation that the change is real, it is happening, and everyone must get on board.

Table 1 | Responsibilities for change

Who	Key responsibilities
Top team	Aligning change with organisational strategy Providing leadership to make change happen Internal and external communication Monitoring and evaluation after implementation
Line management	Owning their part in change Cascading communications Preparing teams for implementation
People management and development professionals and HR functions	Championing the people agenda Redefining the roles, jobs and skills Training and development of staff involved Adapting and refining HR policies – eg careers, rewards Building knowledge and learning on change Communicating and involving staff
Programme and Project Managers (PMs)	Establishing project capability and accountability Communication Management and implementation Project planning Engaging senior management and key stakeholders

Obviously, communication channels must be kept flowing, for there is nothing less inspiring than when leadership is seen by everyone to be 'barking up the wrong tree'. Further, dogmatic approaches to change management – particularly long-term culture change – can isolate people and fail to win the support needed. The top team are ultimately accountable for sign-off of all the change deliverables.

A key enabler of achieving the change has been very high senior management buy-in of the project. That senior management buy-in is absolutely fundamental for the process to work. People cannot easily back out. People need to realise that this is not going to go away.

Process director,
multinational company

Line management

Line managers may or may not be directly involved in project teams concerned with managing for change. In some cases, change projects are staffed almost entirely by external consultants. At other times, change is managed by internal staff seconded to the project. The choice of who should manage change is an important one that can have profound effects on how the change is perceived.

Our findings suggest that change management cannot successfully be outsourced. Incorporating line managers directly on the project team and into the change process is vital to building credibility for and implementing change. A principal responsibility of line management in managing change is ensuring that their teams understand the rationale, nature and implications of the change.

You can have lots of wonderful charts and road maps and stuff like that, but unless people work at the top and cascade down through the line, and they adopt the behaviours and cascade them in turn, change is not going to happen. That's the only way.

Head of strategy,
public sector

HR

Throughout this Briefing, the critical role of HR professionals – specialists and generalists, local and corporate – in successfully managing change

is clear. Strategic and transactional HR brings critical knowledge of the people and wider implications of planned changes. Our surveys identified five key roles for HR:

◻ ensuring that people issues are comprehensively integrated into the change plans and processes

◻ insisting that employee involvement is substantial, not just token

◻ ensuring that the necessary change skills are available to the organisation, when and where it needs them

◻ participating directly themselves at the centre and from the outset of the change process

◻ being ready to seek out wider experience of change and draw upon their own deep experience to enhance learning about change.

> **'Our findings suggest that change management cannot successfully be outsourced.'**

Programme and Project Managers (PMs)

PMs ensure that project capability, plans and resources are in place and used to successfully implement change within the defined project scope. Like other key members in managing for change, they can be drawn from within or outside the organisation. Their role is an extremely critical and demanding one and requires immense skill, experience and support.

Once again, a clear message from both our surveys and the case studies was that good project management was a critical success factor. More than half of the reorganisations in the second survey failed to use disciplined project management techniques, and project management skills were lacking in almost half of all reorganisations (CIPD, 2004).

> **'The overall message seems to be that conceptual knowledge is considered less useful than learning from experience...'**

Consultants

Each of our case studies involved consultants at some phase of change. Nevertheless, our surveys show that experience of consultants is not always positive. The contributions of external consultants to change were regarded as useful by only one third of respondents (CIPD, 2004). The overall message seems to be that conceptual knowledge is considered less useful than learning from experience, although experience from outside organisations is regarded as valuable. The case studies suggest that favourable evaluations of consultants' involvement are more likely where the

consultants bring highly specialised skills that are unlikely to be part of in-house capability. Examples include specific IT knowledge or artistic training and facilitation techniques, and where the consultants tailor their approaches to suit the specific needs of the organisation rather than using generic approaches.

Building the right team

As long as you have the right people on the team, the results will follow. That's why I spend a lot of time on choosing the team. You have to create a developing team with people that will work together.

Change programme director,
multinational company

The above quote is typical in emphasising that the success of change management depends on having the right people, right from the start. Resourcing and bringing on board capable individuals to manage the change is a key contribution of HR professionals. The objectives and scope of the change will influence how it is resourced.

In the following examples we draw upon the case studies to illustrate some of the choices that can be made in pulling together the right team.

Case study 1

Two major independent service companies were to be merged in order to realise financial benefits from harmonising working practices and shared organisational structures. Following announcement of the merger to the City, 40 full-time employees from within both companies were taken off their day-to-day jobs and reassigned to form a defined project team. The project scope and specification was demanding and required enormous commitment and effort:

The team had to set aside any of their own particular preferences, and their particular career aspirations. There was no guarantee at the end of this project that they were going to come out with anything except the experience.

Project manager

The project was delivered on time and to specification in three months. The longer-term implementation proceeded in line with the timetable announced by the chief executive. All the key project team members learnt a great deal from the experience and moved on to rewarding positions in the newly-formed company. Many reported that being involved in the change was a challenge that paid off in career terms.

Case study 2

In contrast to Case study 1, Case study 2 – a fast-moving consumer goods multinational – decided to bring in mostly external resources to facilitate change, explicitly seeking to avoid a defined project-based approach.

This method was decided upon for a number of reasons. First, following a recent major business unit merger, the organisation was in need of some consolidation of cultures, and it was felt that this could not be achieved in too much of a hurry. Second, the organisation felt that it wanted to embed long-term capabilities for change in its people, and that a series of smaller, participatory interventions would be the most appropriate and also a relatively risk-free approach. The importance of a coherent single organisational culture was emphasised against the backdrop of an increasingly tough competitive environment.

We wanted to take people on an organisational journey, to step up their performance, to step up the performance of the business.

Chief executive

Adopting the language of a journey towards a new culture rather than a change project, the top team brought in external expertise to develop a series of events, activities, methods and approaches to bring about the change over a two-year period. Starting with top team workshops and training, there followed a number of workshops and training sessions with each of the work levels, effectively cascading the new ways of working and values through the organisation. In addition, various initiatives were introduced for all staff to volunteer for, including half-day release for all staff to participate in community projects, bringing in artists to challenge people's communication and writing styles, away-days, conferences and meetings.

The training of senior and line managers to cascade new ways of working and behaviours was identified as a key enabler of realising change. The top team recognised that it was crucial to lead by example to enrol all members of the organisation behind a clearly defined vision. The innovative, incremental and creative approach to culture change attracted significant positive publicity in the business press and successfully delivered the required change internally, in terms of business results and positive staff attitudes.

Key messages

◘ Leadership and senior management team sponsorship is crucial.

◘ Strong programme and project management capability is needed.

◘ The contributions of dedicated in-house staff and external consultants must be weighed up and defined.

◘ There is no universally successful approach: change must be tailored to the business needs and culture of the organisation.

Table 2 | Comparison of Case study 1 and 2

Factor	Case study 1: internal	Case study 2: external
Timing	Short time-scale Change must be made quickly Insufficient time to recruit consultants	Long time-scale Change seen as on-going Time to choose the right consultants
Knowledge	Extensive, detailed knowledge of the organisation crucial	Fresh, outside perspectives needed
Capability	Internal capabilities for change management Staff can be seconded	Internal capability for culture change not present Aim to develop internal capability
Stakeholder issues	High risk from stakeholder issues Internal team has credibility and clout	Low risk from stakeholder issues Organisation receptive to outside influences

- Leadership needs to communicate a clear vision of change to the organisation.

- The path to acheiving change should be carefully project-managed.

- Vision and path must remain aligned, and adapt to change.

3 | Crafting the vision and the path

Have a clear view of where you intend to be. Plan and project manage to get there.

Chief executive,
public sector

There are many drivers of change, including technology, competition, regulation and government policy. Organisations have to define how best to organise themselves to effectively respond to these challenges, and build in capability for future change. Most importantly, they need to define how best to realise benefits from the management of change. Change should integrate structures, processes, job design, capabilities and behaviours, in line with the overall strategy. In short, this requires a vision of where the organisation means to get to and a path to get there.

Our case studies and surveys tell us that this principle applies just as much to large-scale changes in global organisations as to change in smaller organisations. Similar processes can be used to define all change activities. Differences do arise in the level of detail required, and getting this right is an important skill. Too much detail chokes a project – paralysis by analysis – whereas too little leads to scope creep and mistakes. The importance of strong internal project management capability cannot be overstated.

In this section we introduce the widely used 'road-map' technique as a tool for developing a change plan. It has been used to great effect in a number of our case studies. Some organisations adapted the road-map principle so it fitted in better with their culture. For example, Case study 4 (on page 15) shows that one organisation used a railway line as a metaphor, with various stations along the way. Another organisation mapped a journey along a curve, with key milestones and events. What they all share is the same principle: a vision of where the organisation requires to be and a path to get there.

> *'Too much detail chokes a project – paralysis by analysis – whereas too little leads to scope creep and mistakes.'*

'Road map' is a process framework that guides change managers through the development of long-term organisation plans. Road map helps managers to:

◻ align organisational design vision with strategy

◻ turn the vision into an evaluated organisation design and capability proposal

◻ develop detailed organisational change plans.

Figure 2 | Road map

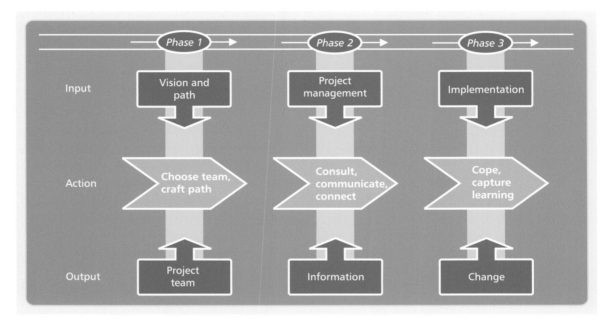

Key steps in the process are outlined in Figure 2.

Features of the road map

There are three clear phases in the process going from vision through to implementation of organisational change. The key steps – inputs, outputs and actions – are all visually linked on one page. These can then be easily cross-referenced to supporting materials and documentation.

Any organisational change can be guided by using the road-map process either in its entirety or by dipping into any one of the key steps. It is important to note that certain essential prerequisites should already be in place. For example, it is a good idea to clarify the vision and the strategy before thinking about organisation design. This may seem obvious, but a number of highly experienced and accomplished practitioners from our case studies warned us that it is an easy and all too common mistake.

To reflect the complexities and changing nature of organisational reality, a road map should be used iteratively, progressively and flexibly rather than treated as a strict linear sequence of actions. Many of our case studies found the road map, or their home-grown versions of it, a useful communication as well as planning tool. Nevertheless, it is important to note that our case study organisations also reported that they were frequently updating and revising their road maps. Making the road map available throughout the organisation via an intranet site, leaflets or posters is an effective communication strategy, but it does have to be in a format that can be updated regularly. An out-of-date road map will send mixed messages and undermine the change agenda. In light of our survey findings that most change initiatives suffered from lack of communication at some stage, this is an important message.

Case study 3

The leadership team of this fast-moving consumer goods multinational recognised that shifting from functional hierarchies to an organisation based on core processes required radical changes to existing behaviours and job roles. Benefits from process and technology implementation would be realised only when people were disciplined about process, understood how what they did related to others, and understood how their role added value. This also meant that the organisation was able to more efficiently exploit redeployed resources.

The most significant challenge facing the project team was the level of co-ordination required within the project. The radical process change was being carried out in business units across the globe. Implementation of the new processes had to be timed very carefully for each of the regions, and business as usual maintained

throughout the preparation, implementation and go-live phases. The international nature of the project also meant that attention had to be paid to cultural differences in the way that the organisation had historically operated – meaning that training and implementation issues would potentially be different at each site.

Communication was a crucial factor to get right in order to make sure that the strategic vision was aligned with the implementation processes. As a process director put it:

We expect each business unit to have a road map aligned with the business strategy. That is a key tool.

Road map supported this alignment by:

◻ aligning project objectives with strategic regional and local business objectives

◻ identifying organisation capability issues

◻ Integrating the project implementation plan within the overall business change agenda.

Case study 4

The transition from being a government department to becoming a competitive commercial organisation required substantial organisation-wide change. In particular, there was a key challenge in communicating the immediate, medium- and long-term strategic vision for the organisation. With an established history of stability and a clear sense of purpose, the move to becoming a leading technology enterprise in a tough market environment was characterised by a shift to more project-based ways of working.

Following extensive and thorough consultations with all levels of employees in the organisation and intensive strategic planning workshops with the senior management team, facilitated by external consultants, an organisational journey was charted. Based on the core principles of road map, the metaphor of a railway journey was developed.

We put this plan together, represented by a railway journey. It's a single-track railway, a one-way journey, because we wouldn't be going back. It didn't have a starting-point because change has been going on forever, and we couldn't say if or when we would finish.

Chief executive

Along the route were 'stations' – key milestones in the organisation's development that could be easily identified. Each of these points had specific actions, inputs and outcomes associated with it, and these had to be completed before the organisation could progress along its journey. The railway journey set out the future vision for the organisation and the means of realising it in a way that was easily communicated throughout the organisation, enabling alignment of the objectives of new projects with the overall strategy.

Key messages

◘ A vision of change must be communicated by the leadership of the organisation.

◘ A path to achieve the change must be set out and carefully project managed.

◘ The vision and path must remain aligned and adapt as the project progresses.

- Processes should be in place to connect and keep track of different dimensions of change.

- Customers and suppliers need to be kept up-to-date with change, and involved, where appropriate.

- Internal resistance to change is often less than anticipated.

4 | Connecting organisation-wide change

You look for people who understand change and change management. They have to be able to make connections, and to think strategically.

HR manager and change director, multinational company

By definition, major change will have an impact throughout the entire organisation. In many cases, changes made to people, processes or technology in one area of the organisation will have knock-on effects in another. A powerful signal coming from our surveys was that changes to people, processes and technology must be connected and integrated across the organisation. The previous chapter showed that a road map is one tool that can help in gaining this holistic, overarching view. Programme and project management capability also supports this approach. In this section we expand the level of detail and present a high-level diagnostic tool to check that change is connected or 'joined-up' across the organisation, as illustrated in Table 3 on page 20.

Design

For change to be successful, the right organisational design is crucial. The design must fit with both the business strategy and the future organisational structures. The time-scale for change must be realistic and achievable, and the human resource implications of the change and the transition period calculated. Further, the design must have sign-off from senior management.

Capability

As change takes place there is a need to consider whether people's existing capability will be sufficient to realise the reorganisation objectives. Training will be needed so that individuals in the organisation understand their role in change and how it will affect them. A plan of action is needed for filling actual and future capability gaps. Our surveys identified some failures in this respect, especially with regard to identifying and developing the required project management skills.

Ways of working

Organisational change by definition brings new ways of working. In our case studies, often this meant a greater emphasis on teamwork and changing individual roles and accountabilities. Individuals may have to become involved in areas previously outside their domain. From a change management point of view, it is important to be confident that the implications of new ways of

Table 3 | Diagnostic for connected change

Dimensions of change	Objective	Evidence of action
Organisation design	Fit with future business structure and strategy Realistic time-scale for implementation Completed gap analysis of existing and new structures	Senior management sign-off
Capability	Comparisons of current and required capabilities Contingency plans for closing capability gaps Development and update of skilling of existing employees Internal or external recruitment	HR documentation
Ways of working	Clarity of new roles and responsibilities Competencies and behaviours required in future defined and communicated New performance criteria understood	Communication and training
Process change	New processes scoped and defined Transition activities planned Plan of action to remove obsolete processes	Project management
Equipment, offices, facilities, physical impact	Accommodation requirements planned Equipment requirements established IT, technology and infrastructure	Facilities management documentation
Risks	Compliance with legal requirements Risk analysis conducted and monitored Contingency plans in place	Legal team sign-off, SMT sign-off
Customers and suppliers	Customers and suppliers consulted Communication channels open	Meetings, away-days, conferences
Assumptions and dependencies	Assumptions and dependencies of change defined Review and monitoring mechanism in place	Documentation

working have been communicated effectively. For the leadership to be seen to adopt the new behaviours early on is an extremely effective strategy in realising this.

Process change

Changes in business processes – for example, procurement, recruitment, reporting and customer relationship management – must be scoped and the timing of their introduction carefully co-ordinated. Very often there are significant IT implications associated with the introduction – and removal – of business processes. It is also extremely important to have a back-up or disaster recovery plan should something go wrong during the transition. A number of our case studies have drawn our attention to how even the smallest hiccup can have potentially serious consequences during business process switching, in one case damaging customer relationships and delivery channels for a lengthy period of time.

Equipment, offices, facilities, physical impacts

Attention to the strategic and business case for a change often shifts attention away from the practical day-to-day implications. Questions of where workstations will be located, where people will have lunch and mix are crucial not just for an effective launch but also for employee buy-in. Many of our case studies that carried out staff consultations identified these issues as key concerns. However, our surveys picked up on the

fact that change managers tend to overestimate the amount of resistance they will meet in this respect. With good communication up front, it may not be as much of a difficulty as is often imagined. Still, from a straightforward operational and logistical point of view, it is important not to underestimate the value of carefully considering requirements for things such as new IT, furniture, software licences, and other materials, and building in realistic delivery and installation times.

> *'It is also extremely important to have a back-up or disaster recovery plan should something go wrong during the transition.'*

Risks

A central challenge in all reorganisation programmes is managing business as usual while undergoing change. Constant assessment of weaknesses and difficulties in the process has to be undertaken in a systematic manner and evaluated in terms of impact on the organisation. Organisational change can have significant effects on a host of regulatory and legal requirements such as health and safety, labelling or details of leases. Change programmes themselves change, and as they do, so too will the risks associated with them.

Customers and suppliers

Customers, suppliers, users and clients must not be forgotten in designing a reorganisation. Both our surveys and case studies highlight that often the concerns of these critical stakeholders are neglected during change. Such important stakeholders must be kept up to date, clear about and comfortable with the changes. Indeed, they may even be able to make some of the changes easier to implement. For example, talking to suppliers about proposals for a new inventory management system could realise benefits for both if the supplier is already operating a compatible stock flow control system. Likewise, communicating proposed changes to recruitment and selection procedures may lead to efficiency gains with recruitment agencies by enabling more focused understanding of requirements.

Assumptions and dependencies

It is crucial to be absolutely clear on the business case assumptions made in planning reorganisation. Plans often change, and when they do, so will the assumptions that underpin them. Effective mechanisms must be in place to capture and communicate these, in order to understand the potential implications. There are a number of mechanisms to enable this, such as keeping a log of change requests to the project, and ensuring that all change requests are signed-off by an appropriate level of management. This also helps keep track of scope creep.

Case study 5

This organisation was more than ready for change as it moved from the public to the private sector. With market-ready cutting-edge technology and high levels of internal capability, it was recognised and widely accepted that traditional ways of working had become obsolete. Moving away from a hierarchical structure to project-based ways of working broke the mould and delivered benefits immediately. However, enthusiasm for project-based ways of working soon created some unforeseen difficulties. Too many projects were being developed in too many different locations in the organisation. Plans were being proposed to co-ordinate projects.

A simple process for project approval was quickly established using the intranet. Here people could view other current projects in the organisation, understand how their ideas connected and how their project might further the vision. Senior management could view the proposal on-line, give approval, and keep track of change across the organisation, avoiding duplication of effort and possible conflicts.

Key messages

◻ There are many dimensions to major organisational change. It is important to make sure that there are processes in place to connect and keep track of them.

◻ Don't forget customers and suppliers. Keep them informed, and they may even be helpful in designing change.

◻ Resistance to change may be less than anticipated. Transparency and good communication from the outset helps get people on board.

- **Effective change is facilitated by stakeholder consultation.**

- **Stakeholder mapping prevents important stakeholders being overlooked.**

- **Proactive stakeholder management is an effective risk management tool.**

5 | Consulting and involving stakeholders

It is the intangible things that businesses have difficulty with. The notion of getting people engaged, getting people interested, and getting people to drive the strategy.

HR manager,
multinational company

Consultation with stakeholders is a key part of implementing successful change, yet is often overlooked due to time and resource pressures. Failure to get stakeholders involved often creates problems. For example, the second survey highlighted that real employee involvement in change can improve results but token involvement is often damaging. Stakeholder management is an area of change where sticking to formulas is unlikely to deliver the best results. Informal approaches to managing stakeholder expectations can often have more impact than formal consultation exercises, at any phase of a reorganisation. This section presents some approaches and lessons from our case studies.

Who are stakeholders?

A stakeholder is anyone who has an interest in the reorganisation or will be affected by it – for example, employees, trade unions, contractors,

customers or suppliers. Understanding the motivations, needs and potential issues that stakeholders might have is a critical success factor in managing change. Indeed, improving stakeholder relationships is often an explicit objective of reorganisations – eg improved customer services.

> **'A stakeholder is anyone who has an interest in the reorganisation or will be affected by it – for example, employees, trade unions, contractors, customers or suppliers.'**

Keeping stakeholders engaged, informed and consulted during the change process requires sustained effort. As mentioned earlier, the surveys and case studies found that customers and suppliers in particular were often left out of consultations. Stakeholder mapping is a useful tool to ensure that all stakeholders have a say in change. (See Figure 3 on page 26.)

The importance of consulting stakeholders

Following the identification of stakeholders through stakeholder mapping it becomes possible

Figure 3 | Stakeholder mapping

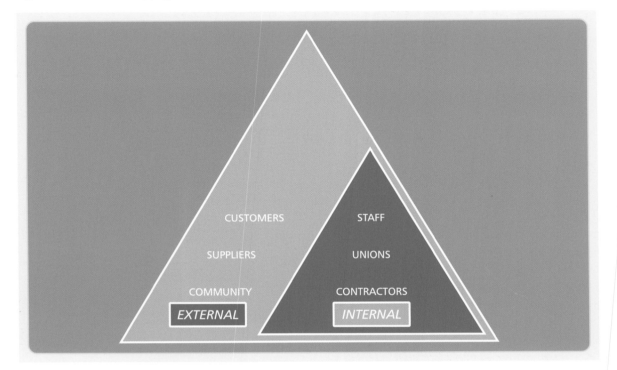

to understand how change is likely to affect them. This understanding makes it easier to manage the influence that stakeholders may exercise over making change happen, including obstructing the process. With careful consideration, potential misunderstandings or conflicts of interest with difficult stakeholders can be avoided.

There are usually many different stakeholders affected by change, to a greater or lesser extent reflecting different motivations and issues at different levels within and outside the organisation. For example, in one of our case studies change managers were simultaneously dealing with a senior management team in flux, a heavily unionised workforce concerned about future job cuts, a new regulatory regime, and customers who were confused about who they were actually buying products and services from. Each of these stakeholders had different perspectives on the change and correspondingly different influences over the rate and direction of change. Through meticulous stakeholder management, employing a wide repertoire of techniques from workshops, away-days, meetings, facilitation and a blend of tried and tested and creative communication techniques, the change managers brought everyone they needed on board to push the change through on time and to specification. However, success in this particular case required substantial effort, time and resources, and it was not always easy. Key groups had to be prioritised and concerns dealt with, and by the right people – accordingly evidenced in the following quote from the change team leader:

It wasn't any of my business to deal with external stakeholders. At the time I was fundamentally involved in consultations with trade unions and communications with employees. I learned a massive amount about the need to communicate, communicate and communicate. That concept forms the grounding for all organisational work I have done after that.The communication, consultation and involvement strategy is what will make it happen.

Delivering change

Achieving change is facilitated by working with stakeholders to agree a clear and realistic set of deliverables. These can be produced through dialogue with stakeholders, and the effort should be made to ensure that each party is clear about what is expected, and when.

Risk management

Not all stakeholders will have positive and constructive attitudes towards change. Indeed, some may be intent on sabotaging change. This can happen at any level. Managing change after a merger, takeover or change in ownership can be especially fraught in this respect. Feelings may be running high at all levels of the organisation, from insecurity about jobs to bitterness about location moves and new ways of working. Using existing knowledge of stakeholder issues it may be possible to anticipate some difficulties. Identification of these issues can form part of the risk management process and inform a counteractive strategy where necessary.

> **'Not all stakeholders will have positive and constructive attitudes towards change. Indeed, some may be intent on sabotaging change.'**

Case study 6

For this organisation, becoming self-funding after being a government agency implied enormous culture change, and potentially enormous opposition from an established local, unionised workforce. The senior management team brought in a team of culture change consultants to establish how stakeholders perceived the organisation. This included staff at all levels, customers, suppliers and the general public. Following the consultants' report, the board decided to host a major event over two days at head office. All 2,000 members of the organisation participated, many of whom had never been there before, despite 20 years of working for the organisation.

The senior management team welcomed everyone and had face-to-face meetings with many. There had never been this level of interaction in the organisation before, marking a radical departure from the remote, hierarchical approach of the past. The workshop was widely acclaimed as a complete success in engaging all stakeholders in the change, breaking down barriers in the organisation:

What this event really did was to move the senior management up in the eyes of the workforce. It helped them understand that there was skill and ability in our senior team, and they were all committing to doing things in a different way and start leading the business more effectively.

Project manager

Feedback on the event from staff was excellent, indicating high levels of enthusiasm for change. Concerns remained about the potential for job losses, but the credibility of the senior management team, and their confidence and concerns for the workforce, had been established. This case study supports the findings from Survey 2 which show that opposition to change is very often not as strong as might be initially anticipated. What is important is how consultation about that change is handled.

Key messages

◘ Consulting stakeholders facilitates the effective design and implementation of change.

◘ Stakeholder mapping ensures that important stakeholders are not left out.

◘ Proactive stakeholder consultation can be an effective risk management tool.

- Effective communication needs to take place at every stage of change.

- Effective communication is consistent, regular and targeted.

- Existing channels of communication should be exploited and new ones developed.

6 | Communicating

Regular, consistent and well-targeted communications are critical to the success of any reorganisation, both to internal and to external stakeholders. The second survey found that reorganisations accompanied by more extensive communications with external stakeholders are linked to better performance outcomes. The previous chapter emphasised that engaging and informing all those affected by the implications of a major project is an important challenge. There is a range of activities that have to take place at different phases of a change programme to ensure effective communication.

◘ *Contact*: Two-way flows of communication between the change team and stakeholders have to be established. Information must also be organised and effectively managed if it is to fulfil its potential. The most appropriate tools, techniques and methods for engaging different stakeholders have to be considered.

Figure 4 | The COMS communication cycle

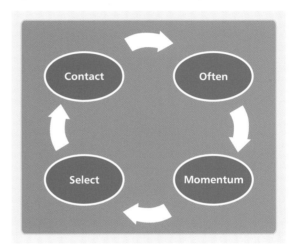

◘ *Often*: A key success factor is maintaining regular communications. This can be via weekly meetings, daily briefs, monthly newsletters, frequent e-mails - whatever is appropriate and effective. Maintaining regular communications makes change real, familiar and personal. Looking for opportunities to deliver messages to key stakeholders is important. Existing channels of communications can be expanded and new ones created. Reviewing the messages and channels used ensures that they remain effective and relevant.

◘ *Momentum*: During this phase the change starts to take place. Maintaining momentum of communications is critical at this time as people start to see and feel the change. Communication must be kept regular, accurate and transparent, and it must run smoothly and effectively. It is important both to keep talking and keep listening, as well as evaluating. In larger programmes where implementation may be phased, it is often helpful to share experiences across the organisation of where change has gone well and to capture learning.

◘ *Select*: In the lead-up to and immediately after the change 'go-live' there will be increased demand for information about the success, challenges and learning from implementation efforts. What is the best tone, nature and frequency of communication activity to select will depend on the profile, risk and subsequent per-formance of the 'go-live'. The options range from special, one-off briefings or newsletters to weekly progress reports or even 'business as usual' updates as part of other regular business matters.

> **'Users, management and other stakeholders will demand honest, consistent and up-to-date information whether the news is good, bad or unremarkable.'**

It is very likely that most change initiatives will experience some teething problems in the early days. Users, management and other stakeholders will demand honest, consistent and up-to-date information whether the news is good, bad or unremarkable.

Case study 7

The communication was one of the most important things for getting this programme out of the doldrums.

Change programme manager,
retailer

This high-street retailer's head office had developed a deeply entrenched culture that was resistant to and sceptical of change. Overcoming this scepticism presented major communications challenges. First, clear communication channels were set up between the project team and the senior management team. This meant regular, scheduled, quality 'air time' with the project sponsor and a steering group. Meetings were held every two weeks, with reports that followed a standard format and were circulated to all members several days in advance. One-off communication events were held with the senior managers, showing them around the new building and mock-ups of new office space. This very quickly had a positive effect:

After about two or three months we had improved the relationship between the [project] team and the steering group. The steering group felt more comfortable and more confident in the ability of the team to deliver.

Change programme manager

Positive communication about change was directed to all parts of the organisation. A whole range of tools and techniques were used to ensure that this happened. A communications room, intranet sites, newsletters and information sessions were all arranged. Regular staff surveys were conducted assessing the awareness of the project and attitudes towards it. Change team managers were appointed for each department as points of contact for employees to keep up to date with the change programme.

Key messages

◻ An effective communications strategy is important at each phase of change, and should be easily recognised and understood by internal and external stakeholders.

◻ Effective communications are consistent, regular and targeted. Sustaining this requires dedicated resources.

◻ The involvement of communications professionals often delivers a better strategy than the use of in-house resources by bringing in external experience, creativity and knowledge of a wider variety of tools.

◻ Existing channels of communication should be exploited, and new ones developed. HR can be a key resource in identifying these channels.

- Managing change and 'business as usual' at the same time can be stressful.

- Strong leadership and listening skills are needed to ensure stakeholder concerns are addressed.

- Legitimate concerns, especially around work–life balance, must be seriously addressed. Token gestures can backfire.

7 | Coping with change

Make sure that you deal with the soft issues as well as the hard issues on the way, because the organisation's surviving and [your] managing your business afterwards is the objective.

Change programme director,
service sector multinational company

Change does not happen from plans alone, and when change is happening, the organisation has to continue functioning and meeting its day-to-day responsibilities. This dual responsibility can be the source of enormous stress for many. Doing something and changing how you do it at the same time is no mean feat and should not be underestimated. In particular, introducing change can create tension with line management who are working full-time to their business-as-usual objectives. One approach to relieving this tension is to allocate dedicated resources to work full-time on change. As one experienced change manager in our case studies put it:

If you are going to source your project team internally, they should be taken right off their day jobs to work on a programme. That's how it should work.

Where changes are more incremental, with longer time frames and perhaps less driven by crisis, it is possible to strike a balance between full-time dedicated project teams and allocating a percentage of people's time. This observation relates back to the skills needed to choose the right project team for the job. In this section we draw on the experience of 'battle-hardened' practitioners from our case studies and present a collection of views and strategies on how to get through these testing times of change.

It's not just the plan...

'Doing something and changing how you do it at the same time is no mean feat and should not be underestimated.'

Although project plans, road maps and process charts are important tools for change, they need physical action to make them happen. This is particularly important when the plans require people to adopt new working practices. New working practices and behaviours often require a change in attitudes – people have to be persuaded of the value of the new organisational agenda.

Perhaps the most difficult aspect of any change management programme is meeting existing business requirements that have to be reconciled with the change requirements at a future point in time. This can be incredibly demanding on individuals, and if not recognised, can lead to severe morale and motivation problems. Change plans can themselves change for any number of reasons, internal or external. Effective change managers are able to adapt to shifting circumstances and identify potential changes in course sooner rather than later – ie they are flexible, and do not simply implement plans regardless of changing circumstances.

> *'Effective change managers are able to adapt to shifting circumstances and identify potential changes in course sooner rather than later...'*

Effective change managers

Effective change managers face a tough task. They have to understand the current organisational situation well and be able to connect this with the planned change. They must be able to communicate the case for change to diverse stakeholders, highlighting how the change will affect them. This involves acknowledging past achievements and efforts and building on existing strengths within the organisation. Effective communication is critical, as is good judgement of the time-scales involved.

In our case studies, effective change managers have been those who are able to show people what the new organisation will 'look and feel' like and demonstrate how it will support the business objectives. In one case, this involved building mock-ups of new office spaces and workstations. Pointing to concrete examples of where change has already taken place in different parts of the organisation, particularly in large-scale change programmes, is also a very useful technique.

Coping with 'the change roller-coaster'

The way that individuals respond to change has been well researched. Individuals pass through a cycle of emotions as they deal with change and its consequences. The timing and depth of the experiences differ between individuals but tend to follow the same pattern. Described by a change manager from one of our case studies as a 'roller-coaster', the cycle is shown in Figure 5, opposite.

◘ *immobilisation*: This is the initial feeling of being 'stunned' and may last for just a moment or continue for some time.

◘ *denial*: People who disagree with any aspect of the change will spend longer in denial than those who see change as positive. Typically, those in denial will behave as if nothing has changed or is going to change.

◘ *anger*: Although anger can be expressed in a number of ways, in the context of the change

Figure 5 I The change cycle

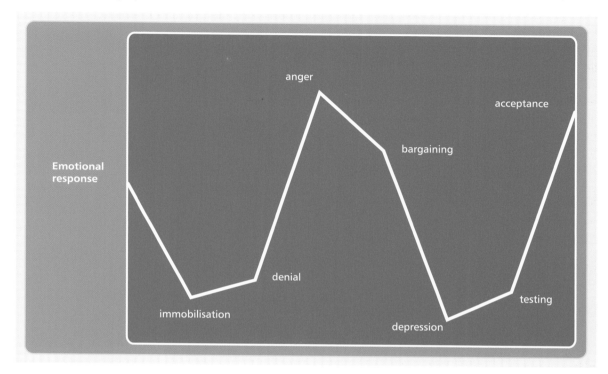

cycle it signifies that people have acknowledged the change.

- *bargaining*: Impacts of the change have been recognised and people begin to consider alternatives.

- *depression*: Nostalgia for the old ways of doing things and old relationships takes hold. Where radical change has taken place, this phase may take a long time to pass.

- *testing*: People buy in to the change and start challenging and testing the change under different scenarios.

- *acceptance*: The change is finally embraced and people work together to make it happen, even if some still disagree with the rationale for it.

Helping others make change happen

Of course people worry about how change will affect them, particularly if they are not involved in its development. However, as mentioned earlier, our surveys show that initially at least people can be enthusiastic about change. It is crucially important that the change team or communications people within it provide relevant, meaningful information about the change. In particular, communication with line management can play a key role by acting as effective conduits to ensure that correct information is passed on. In this way people do not have to rely on rumours or false information about the change. Change managers must keep up to date and remain transparent about developments.

> **'Uncertainty about change...may lead to increased absenteeism and have a negative impact on the home lives of colleagues.'**

Uncertainty about change can lead to stress and anxiety that in turn can lead to people having difficulty thinking clearly, making sound decisions or being creative. More seriously, it may lead to increased absenteeism and have a negative impact on the home lives of colleagues. For example, people may feel that they are required to work longer hours, missing time with their families, in order to meet the requirements of their day jobs and the demands of being involved in driving a change project through. Even full-time change team resources can experience this:

My overriding memory of the project is things like getting to half past seven at night and the leader saying, 'Right – what do you want from Burger King? We are not going anywhere.' Long days and late nights because we had drawn this line in the sand and we were going to do it. A huge personal commitment from the team.

Change team member,
service sector

Individuals have different stress thresholds. Some people perform well under pressure and conditions of change, finding it rewarding:

It's good to be able to get people on board and say 'I want you to work really, really hard for the next three months, burning the midnight oil, round the clock – and by the way, you won't have a job at the end of it.'

Change team leader,
retail

Others become anxious about what may appear to be only minor changes in conditions. Even in supportive environments, people may disguise their true feelings of cynicism or denial. Effective change managers ensure that concerns are listened to carefully, and that people feel that they can be heard. One technique for ensuring that this happens is to have regular meetings both with those implementing the change and with those affected by it. Once again, the importance of genuine two-way communication is emphasised.

Case study 8

Introducing radical change in this specialised education agency was an extremely sensitive matter. Faced with an increasingly aggressive and competitive marketplace, as well as tightening regulation, ways of working that had been in place for 40 years had to change. A loyal, unified and local workforce was the strength of the organisation although it had always had an adversarial relationship with management. People were deeply anxious about job reallocation and specification. Persuading staff that change was not about redundancy but about re-training, career development and the survival of the organisation was key to the success... but a very difficult process.

When I came in, it was all positive, positive, positive. We all want this change. Everyone was singing from the same hymnsheet. But in reality, what really surprised me was the depth and severity of how resistant people were. They were paying lip service in terms of commitment – let's go along with this. But the underhand tactics and the backstabbing politics that came through were really quite frightening, really quite staggering.

HR manager

Further, there was also resistance from the management team to the changes.

I was also experiencing resistance within the management team. So although we were chipping away at this iceberg – well, it is more like holding an avalanche, really, because you kind of shore that bit up and then this bit slips down, you know – it is just hard work.

The turning-point was reached by a change in approach from the change team. First, they adopted a new leadership style.

We took on this new assertive kind of stance. This is the Board of Trustees directive, this is the independent business review, and this is what we are going to do. We just started pushing and pushing. Once the momentum got going again, everybody rallied behind it.

Next, the change team started using a range of tools, techniques and methods to introduce discrete pieces of change incrementally. This included training on new IT systems, consultation away-days, workshops, and bringing in external facilitators and trainers. Staff slowly started to engage with the changes, tangibly demonstrating that change would benefit them, provided that they supported it, and also that ultimately there was no choice:

If we didn't do it, we would be swallowed up by one of the big boys and incorporated with one of our competitors. We would lose our independence and autonomy.

Change team leader

Key messages

◘ Making change happen and managing business as usual can be stressful. Choose the team carefully and consider full-time dedicated resources.

◘ Effective change managers can anticipate and respond to the different phases of the change cycle by listening to stakeholder concerns – but strong leadership is also needed.

◘ Communication, including listening, can help people through the change cycle. Legitimate concerns and worries must be acknowledged and responded to, particularly those that impact on work–life balance. Token gestures may backfire.

- **Previous experience of change is a key resource and should be engaged.**

- **Capturing learning is an efficient risk management tool.**

- **HR professionals play a vital role in capturing learning.**

8 | Capturing learning

Instead of going in and asking the question 'What went wrong?', I went in and asked the question 'What works well?'

Change team leader,
multinational company

Our surveys and case studies strongly emphasise that systematically capturing learning from key stages in a reorganisation is a vital prerequisite of developing a capability to reorganise on a regular basis successfully. Sharing and applying these insights and experiences reduces time and resources that might have been spent on reinventing the wheel. Planning and decision-making are improved and future chances of project success are also improved. Repetition of expensive mistakes can be avoided. In this section we illustrate some mechanisms for capturing learning from change.

Learning is any significant insight or knowledge gained during a project that can be applied elsewhere at some other time. Sharing knowledge of this kind throughout an organisation significantly increases the chances of success for future initiatives. Further, sharing learning can help to develop an open, more supportive communication culture that is essential for continuous improvement.

Sharing learning can also help create more realistic assessments of benefits from change. In the survey we found too many examples of a lack of learning from past experiences internally or from the experiences of other organisations. Too often the design of changes was in the hands of a small minority, sometimes applying a solution used elsewhere and without tailoring to the specific needs and circumstances of the current organisation.

It is also important to encourage improvements or reinforce successes. Figure 6 shows that capturing learning can be seen as a four-stage process.

- *Look*: Gather information and observations about what happened from different perspectives. Draw up a picture and an accurate, coherent storyline. Consider what might have been done differently and how this would have made a difference to outcomes. Note what could be done differently in the future.

- *Think*: Try to understand what happened and identify people, process or technology issues that enabled or constrained change. Identification of key leverage points in influencing change is useful for possible future interventions.

◘ *Act*: Having identified what might have been done differently, and the enablers and constraints of change, work out what can be done straight away to implement the lessons. Identify who needs to take the necessary decisions and establish the business case for implementing learning. A straightforward approach is to rank all possible corrective actions by the size of benefit versus the difficulty of implementation. Agree and set implementation goals.

◘ *Review actions*: The key question to ask here is whether or not the desired changes have been achieved. If not, evaluate what must be changed. Begin the cycle of learning again.

Figure 6 | Capturing learning

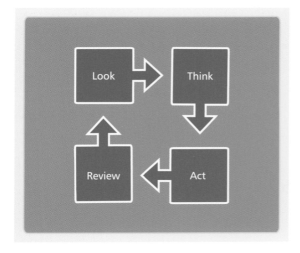

Capture learning

Learning can be experienced at any phase of change and, as a result, should be captured at any time. The amount of time and resources directed at capturing learning should be proportional to the amount of value it generates for the project or organisation – for example, tangible improvements to working practices or risk reduction. A number of our case studies have emphasised that it is good practice to conduct regular, low-key learning activity. This could be at weekly project meetings and/or at the end of discrete project phases when milestones are reached. It helps to keep the project on track in terms of whether or not the goals are being achieved. More extensive formal reviews should also be conducted periodically, particularly after the reorganisation 'go-live'.

Connect learning to project and risk management

Not all of the lessons learned can be resolved or incorporated into the organisation in a single step. Learning that may have a significant impact on the reorganisation project – or on future initiatives – can be recorded within a projects risk/action register and maintained by the person responsible for project risk management. At each phase in the project where this particular risk has relevance, it is the joint responsibility of the risk manager, project manager and milestone owner to agree how they will address, mitigate or eliminate this risk.

HR's role in capturing learning

A key role for HR professionals is developing processes to import and capture learning. They can also arrange provision, as well as receiving training themselves, in organisational development and change management to relevant staff within the organisation.

Case study 9

This fast-moving consumer goods multinational was rolling out complex and comprehensive business process change across five global regions. It was recognised early on that important lessons could be learned from each implementation that could be carried forward to the next. Processes and procedures were put in place for teams to visit sites that had 'gone-live' in order to capture their experiences. In addition, managers that had taken their business units through implementation travelled to sites that were preparing to go-live. Lessons were documented and circulated as an effective means of risk reduction.

One of the key enablers of the learning was the encouragement of an open, transparent, 'no-blame' culture. This was achieved by treating learning as a positive outcome of experience that should be valued and passed on to others in the organisation that were about to go through similar processes. It was also facilitated by senior management taking responsibility and being accountable for implementation. Otherwise, people were inclined to keep potential issues and problems to themselves, rather than regarding them as a challenge for the organisation and something their colleagues would be interested in finding out about.

A number of our case study organisations have developed effective mechanisms for capturing learning, including intranet sites for people to share information and training programmes to encourage people to be more open and critically supportive of colleagues.

> *'Learning can be experienced at any phase of change and, as a result, should be captured at any time.'*

Key messages

◘ Learning should take place at each phase of change.

◘ Previous experience of making change happen is a key resource.

◘ Capturing learning is an efficient risk management tool.

◘ Establishing and managing these learning processes is a key role of the HR professional.

- **HR plays a positive role in relation to every dimension of making change happen.**

- **HR is best placed to build the capability for sustainable change in organisations.**

- **HR plays an increasingly strategic role in change management.**

9 | HR: making change happen

My roles in the project were multiple. [They were] to make sure that the people agenda was addressed. To make sure that a balance was struck between ruthless efficiency and the needs of the people.

Group HR director,
service organisation

Choosing a team: being a team

Making change happen requires a sophisticated mix of skills. Leadership, senior management, line management, HR and internal and external consultants all play key roles.

The survey findings demonstrated that a significant level of involvement of HR professionals differentiated successful changes from less successful ones, and also demonstrated a growing influence of HR professionals within change. However, there remains a need for HR to grasp the chance to move away from a retrospective clearing-up role to one where involvement in change is a key component of the HR role.

The case studies and surveys emphasised the importance of HR professionals not only in ensuring that the right skills were available when the organisation needed them, but also in participating as a critical member of the change team. At a transactional level, HR can support leadership in choosing the right team and operationally in developing revised job designs, recruitment procedures, and other processes that are needed in the new organisation. The skills of operational HR are also essential for identifying training needs, capability gaps and calculating workable time-scales. From a transformational perspective, HR's role includes:

- emphasising the 'people' goals of the change instead of only the narrower and short-term demands

- building the capability to reorganise throughout the organisation.

> *'HR [needs] to...move away from a retrospective clearing-up role to one where involvement in change is a key component...'*

Crafting the vision and the path

HR must be involved early on in the visioning processes – a point emphasised by several of our case studies and not lost on most chief executives, according to the surveys. Strategic vision without understanding the people implications is likely to prove unworkable at best and plain risky at worst. When it comes to building the path for change, HR is ideally placed to input into the road map, providing essential information regarding recruitment, appointments, capability and training needs analyses. In addition, HR can assess the time-scales for implementation across the organisation in light of the required consultations with various stakeholders.

Connecting organisation-wide change

HR is a central function in connecting organisation-wide change. Organisation design, capability gaps, training needs and new ways of working and facilities planning are all linked to people issues. Consequently, HR should be able to develop a perspective on how changes made in one part of an organisation will enable or constrain change in another. This also applies to external relationships with customers and suppliers.

Consulting stakeholders

Chapter 5 explored the role of stakeholder consultation in making change happen. Identified very strongly by the surveys as a critical success factor, this is yet another area where HR has a wealth of experience and skill to draw upon. In many ways, HR is constantly engaged in negotiating with a significant array of organisational stakeholders as part of 'business as usual'. This constant engagement provides HR with a deep knowledge of stakeholder concerns. Such knowledge enables potential stakeholder issues to be ironed out before they become problematic. HR thus plays a key role in risk reduction in this respect, in addition to its engagement role.

Communicating

Although internal communications is becoming an increasingly important role of HR, it is the responsibility of all those involved in change to communicate their activities throughout the organisation, including upwards and outwards. As mentioned previously, HR is well placed to understand the optimal forms of communication with different stakeholders and to understand some of the potential sensitivities that might arise in communication. To this extent, HR can play a vital part, whether in partnership with a communications team or on its own. Further, given the finding from the survey that points to the importance of effective people management in making change happen, particularly in communicating potential changes to people's working conditions, HR has a role in making the implications of change clear to those affected by it. The way to do this was neatly put by an HR director in one of our case studies:

Well, the lesson I learned was that you had to use every medium that was available to you, and exploit all the channels.

Coping with change

As people move through the change cycle, so their morale, motivation and commitment change. Uncertainty about future job prospects and ways of working takes its toll, sometimes leading to increased absenteeism or underperformance. These are clearly HR issues, and issues that HR is greatly experienced in coping with. Managing people through the change cycle, maintaining motivation under difficult circumstances and making the change happen is a major responsibility that HR professionals are well equipped to deal with. People can be engaged through various kinds of communication – e-mail, newsletters, meetings, workshops and intranet sites.

Capturing learning

HR is well situated not just to capture its own learning from change – a valuable strength in this area – but also to capture the learning of others. By being able to show how various policies and procedures facilitated or impacted change, HR can design processes and systems that take this into account. Cross-functional strategic thinking, the holistic view mentioned earlier, allows broader lessons to be incorporated into the organisation.

Case study 10

Organisational change is more than just re-drawing the lines and the boxes.

HR director,
service sector.

HR played a transformational role in the planning and delivery of a merger of two very large service businesses over a two-year period. HR supported strategic, operational and transactional aspects at each stage. The organisation was fortunate in that it had significant project management experience and resources in-house. However, HR provided a critical role in helping strike the optimal balance between the more operational aspects of reorganisation and the people issues, as the following quote illustrates:

The danger was that our project managers – very good at the nuts and bolts stuff – managed the projects but ignored some of the softer issues. As HR, we built in a dedicated people stream for the appointments activity and the communications activity. Changing the organisation systems and processes has to be done alongside addressing the people issues of the transition.

HR manager,
change project team

As the second survey reports show, the contribution HR experience can make is highly valued on reorganisation projects. The project director in this case study made the following observation:

But I knew that the better the process got handled in people terms, the more likely it would be that the results would be achieved because people wouldn't feel as if they had been treated badly on the way to their new organisation. My experience told me that doing the right thing here minimises disruption downstream. People will accept organisational changes if they feel they have had a fair crack of the whip. If you make partisan and secret appointment decisions, the reaction from people will be off the scales. Managing and mitigating the effects of all that is disastrous. That's why you need HR.

References

GOOLD, M. and CAMPBELL, A. (2002)

Designing Effective Organizations: How to create structured networks. Jossey-Bass.

KUBLER-ROSS, E. (1969)

On Death and Dying. New York: Collier, Macmillan Publishing.

WHITTINGTON, R. and MAYER, M. (2002)

Organising For Success in the Twenty-First Century: A starting point for change. London: CIPD.

CHARTERED INSTITUTE OF PERSONNEL AND DEVELOPMENT (2003)

Reorganising for Success: CEOs' and HR managers' perceptions. Survey report. London: CIPD. Also available online at: www.cipd.co.uk/surveys

CHARTERED INSTITUTE OF PERSONNEL AND DEVELOPMENT (2004)

HR and Reorganisation – Managing the challenge of change. Change Agenda. London: CIPD. Also available online at: www.cipd.co.uk/changeagendas

CHARTERED INSTITUTE OF PERSONNEL AND DEVELOPMENT (2004)

Reorganising for Success: A survey of HR's role in change. Survey report. London: CIPD. Also available online at: www.cipd.co.uk/surveys